GRADE 3

FLASH FORWARD MATH

Written by **Shannon Keeley**

Illustrations by **Jannie Ho**

D1495813

© 2007 by Flash Kids

Cover illustration by John Haslam

All rights reserved. No part of this publication may be reproduced,
stored in a retrieval system, or transmitted, in any form or by any means,
electronic, mechanical, photocopying, recording, or otherwise,
without prior written permission from the publisher.

Flash Kids
A Division of Barnes & Noble
122 Fifth Ave
New York, NY 10011

ISBN: 978-1-4114-0639-1

Please submit all inquiries to FlashKids@bn.com

Printed and bound in Canada

Lot #:
11 13 15 17 16 14 12 10
02/13

Dear Parent,

Math can be one of the most difficult subjects for young learners. Your child may not fully grasp concepts such as long division, multiplication with carrying, or word problems—even with a great math teacher and a thorough math textbook. Here to help at home are almost 100 pages of short drills and fun games that will reinforce all math skills taught in the third grade.

This colorful workbook focuses on your child's competence in multiplication, division, place value, ordering numbers, probability, fractions, and decimals. He or she will also get practice with triangle types, estimating, measurement, volume, area, and perimeter. Additionally, activities with tables and charts keep your child engaged.

The activities are designed for your child to handle alone, but you can read along and help with any troublesome concepts. Together you can check answers at the back of the workbook, and you should always give praise and encouragement for his or her effort. In addition, try to find ways to show your child how these number skills apply to everyday situations. For example, ask him or her to multiply or divide simple household objects, such as crayons or magnets; make a table to show the family's weekly schedule; identify and count triangle types spotted during a car trip or walk around the neighborhood; or determine the correct bills and coins needed to buy an item at a store. Use your imagination!

Place Value Placemats

Look at the underlined numeral on each plate. Draw a line to the placemat with the correct place value. The first one is done for you.

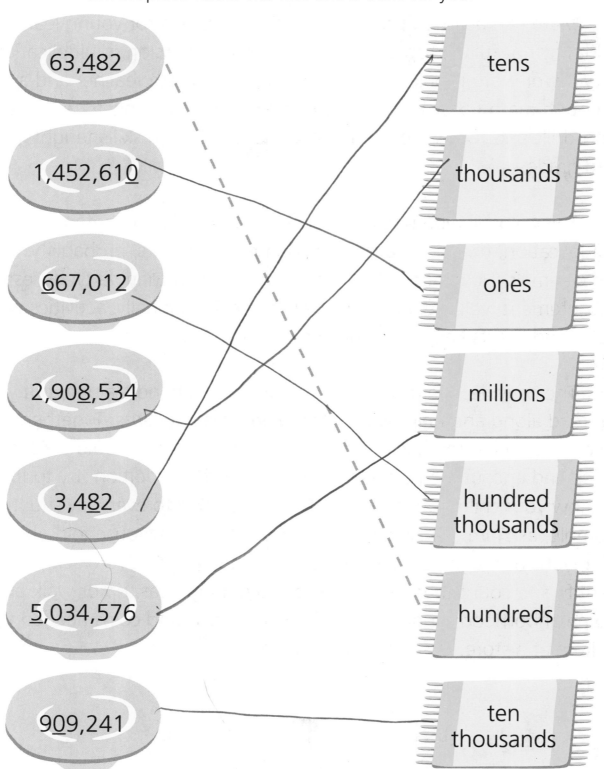

63,4<u>8</u>2

1,452,61<u>0</u>

<u>6</u>67,012

2,9<u>0</u>8,534

3,4<u>8</u>2

<u>5</u>,034,576

9<u>0</u>9,241

tens

thousands

ones

millions

hundred thousands

hundreds

ten thousands

Zero Gravity

Find the zero in each number and write the place value it holds on the line.
The first one is done for you.

1. 65,780
_____ones_____

2. 3,105
_____tens_____

3. 8,064,921
_____hundred thousand_____

4. 30,416,734
_____millions_____

5. 660,732
_____thousand_____

6. 42,012
_____hundreds_____

Write each phrase or equation as a number.
There will be a zero in each number.

7. 6 hundreds, 2 ones _____602_____

8. 500 + 20 _____520_____

9. 3 thousands, 5 hundreds, 7 ones _____3507_____

10. 400 + 5 _____405_____

11. 4 ten thousands, 6 thousands, 8 tens, 3 ones _____46083_____

12. 20,000 + 300 + 90 + 4 _____20,394_____

Ready Race

Compare each pair of numbers along the racetrack. Write **<**, **>**, or **=** in each circle. Count the number of times each symbol appears and write the totals on the cars below. The car with the highest number wins the race!

START

1. 33,856 ◯ 38,356

2. 5 ones ◯ 5 tens

3. 435 ◯ 4 hundreds, 3 tens, 5 ones

4. 9,415,870 ◯ 9,475,870

5. 576 ◯ 516

6. 1 ten ◯ 10 ones

7. 8,010 ◯ 8,001

8. 2 tens, 5 ones ◯ 250

9. 44,073 ◯ 4,703

FINISH

10. 4 hundreds, 2 tens, 8 ones ◯ 4 thousands, 2 hundreds

Merry Go Rounding

Write the rounded number on the line.

1. Round 439 to the nearest ten. _____

2. Round 2,108 to the nearest hundred. _____

3. Round 88,740 to the nearest ten thousand. _____

4. Round 63,805 to the nearest thousand. _____

5. Round 307,986 to the nearest hundred thousand. _____

6. Round 5,783,013 to the nearest million. _____

Look at each pair of numbers. The second number has been rounded. Write the place value the second number was rounded to. The first problem is done for you.

7.   316   320

_____tens_____

8.   4,312   4,310

_____

9.   638   600

_____

10.   25,891   26,000

_____

11.   2,439   2,400

_____

12.   72,434   72,430

_____

Follow the Fox Trail

Start in the middle of the maze and follow the number trails. Find the trail with numbers listed from least to greatest. The word at the end of the correct trail completes the sentence below.

herd

bale

4,047

4,740

4,896

4,689

4,698

4,704

4,986

4,407

4000

4,150

4,024

4,105

4,240

4,510

4,051

4,420

4,402

pride

skulk

A group of foxes is called a _____.

Carnival Count

Read each problem and solve it.

1. The carnival was open Monday through Friday. On Monday, 2,408 people came. There were 2,804 people there on Tuesday. On Wednesday 2,084 people visited, and on Thursday there were 2,480 people. On Friday, 2,840 people visited. Write the days of the week in order from the greatest number of visitors to the least.

_____

_____

_____

_____

2. During the week, the carnival snack bar sold 5,076 hot dogs and 5,067 burgers. It also sold 5,760 cookies and 5,607 ice cream bars. That same week, 6,075 popsicles were sold. Write the snack bar foods in order from the least popular to the most popular.

_____

_____

_____

_____

_____

3. On Wednesday, 339 people rode the super slide. The fun house was visited by 452 people. On the Ferris wheel there were a total of 412 riders. When rounded to the nearest hundred, which attraction had 400 people ride it?

_____

4. The clown sold 88 red balloons, 47 blue balloons, 129 yellow balloons, and 153 green balloons. If you round each number to the nearest hundred, which colors round to 100 balloons?

_____

How High?

Write each expanded notation problem as a number to show the height of each landmark.

1. 1,000 + 200 + 50

_____ feet

2. 1,000 + 600 + 60 + 7

_____ feet

3. 3,000 + 600 + 60 + 6

_____ inches

4. 10,000 + 1,000 + 800 + 30 + 2

_____ inches

Write each number in expanded notation.

5. Mount Everest: 29,035 feet

_____ + _____ + _____ + _____

6. Mount McKinley: 20,320 feet

_____ + _____ + _____

Expanding Equations

Write each number in expanded notation.

1. 4,658 _____

2. 33,450 _____

3. 806 _____

4. 126,800 _____

5. 24,027 _____

6. 590,602 _____

Circle the number that equals the expanded notation equation.

7. 7,000 + 300 + 40 + 2   73,420   734   7,342

8. 500 + 20 + 8   528   582   5208

9. 30,000 + 200 + 10 + 9   32,190   30,219   32,109

10. 1,000 + 80 + 6   186   1,086   1,860

11. 40,000 + 300 + 90 + 6   4,396   141,369   40,396

12. 60,000 + 1,000 + 400 + 30   61,430   6,143   60,143

Jelly Bean Jar

This giant jar holds thousands of jellybeans! The chart shows how many jellybeans of each flavor are in the jar. Use the chart to answer the questions below.

Grape	1,018
Banana	1,081
Vanilla	811
Berry	801
Apple	1,810
Coconut	108

1. List the flavors from the greatest to least number of jellybeans.

_____ _____ _____

_____ _____ _____

2. How many flavors have the numeral 1 in the tens place? _____

3. Which flavors have more than 1,000 jellybeans in the jar?

_____ _____ _____

4. Which flavors have less than 1,000 jellybeans in the jar?

_____ _____ _____

5. If you round all of the flavors to the nearest thousand, how many round to 1,000?_____

Special Delivery

Last year, the local post office delivered lots of cards for the holidays. For Valentine's Day, 20,349 cards were delivered. Around Mother's Day 34,819 cards were delivered. On Father's Day, the post office delivered 7,376 cards. Round each number to the nearest ten thousand. Make a bar on the graph showing the rounded number for each holiday.

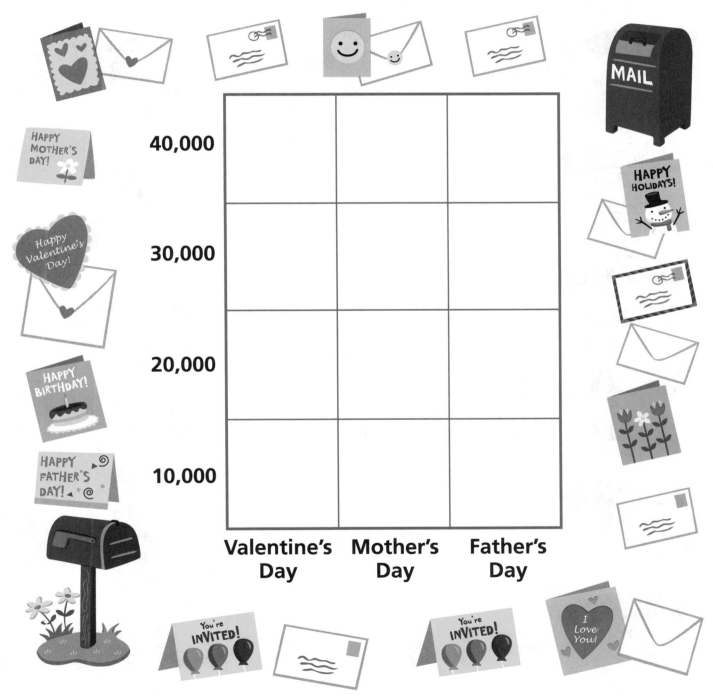

All-Star Addition Match!

Solve the addition problems inside the jerseys and the balls. Draw a line to match the problems that have the same sum.

12
+ 6

24
+ 3

35
+ 4

10
+ 18

22
+ 14

31
+ 5

4
+ 15

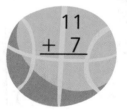
11
+ 7

15
+ 13

15
+ 30

20
+ 7

16
+ 3

42
+ 3

31
+ 8

Triple Tricks

Add to solve each problem.

1.   4
     3
  + 2

2. 203
    + 84

3.   1
     8
  + 5

4. 317
    + 62

5. 3 + 2 + 6 =

6. 452
    + 314

7.   9
     0
  + 7

8.   75
    + 812

9. 8 + 3 + 4 =

10. 724
     + 173

11. 10
     4
   + 3

12. 515
     + 461

Table for Ten

Add each number with the value at the top of the table. Write the sum on the right.
Complete all ten tables on both pages.

+ 3	
5	
4	
3	
7	
9	

+ 7	
6	
2	
1	
9	
5	

+ 1	
8	
3	
4	
7	
9	

+ 5	
0	
6	
4	
5	
8	

+ 2	
9	
1	
2	
4	
3	

+ 4	
2	
6	
9	
3	
4	

+ 0	
8	
1	
7	
0	
5	

+ 6	
3	
9	
6	
2	
7	

+ 9	
7	
2	
9	
4	
5	

+ 8	
9	
8	
5	
3	
0	

The Total Trail

Find the trail that leads through the maze to the exit. Then add together all the numbers along the trail. Remember to regroup. Circle the sign at the end that shows the sum of all the numbers on the trail.

START

13

24

18

51

44

28

33

35

40

63

52

26

166   168   144   179

Regroup Ranch

Add to solve the problems. Remember to regroup.

1. 135
  + 28

2. 56
  + 77

11
246
+ 85
331

3. 18
  + 358

4. 406
  + 96

5. 75
  + 75

6. 474
  + 58

7. 106
  + 394

8. 290
  + 571

9. 509
  + 222

10. 787
  + 363

11. 309
  + 299

12. 547
  + 349

What's the ADDress?

Solve the addition problems. Write the sum to complete the address for each famous place.

1. 654 + 946 =

_____ Pennsylvania Avenue

The White House, Washington D.C.

2. 38 + 72 + 96 =

_____ Sixth Avenue

The Space Needle,
Seattle, Washington

3. 84 + 108 + 108 =

_____ Alamo Plaza

The Alamo
San Antonio, Texas

4. 116 + 117 =

_____ South
Wacker Drive

The Sears Tower,
Chicago, Illinois

5. 500 + 365 + 448 =

_____ Harbor Blvd

This is the address for Disneyland
in Anaheim, California!

6. 42 + 75 + 122 =

_____ Arch Street

In Philadelphia, Pennsylvania, this is
the home where Betsy Ross lived.

The Addition Magician

Solve the problems.

1. There were three magic shows over the weekend. On Friday night, 153 people came to see the show. At the Saturday matinee there were 142 people, and on Saturday night 265 people came to the show. How many people came to the shows altogether?

_____

2. The Addition Magician did a trick where he turned one caterpillar into 78 butterflies. Then, another 99 butterflies flew out of his hat. There were also 63 dragon flies in his magic hat. How many butterflies were used in the trick altogether?

_____

3. After the magic show, the Addition Magician always signs 45 autographs. There were three shows over the weekend. How many autographs did he sign in all?

_____

4. The Addition Magician has a set of magic cards. In the deck he has 37 hearts, 28 spades, 35 clubs, and 22 diamonds. How many total cards are in the deck?

_____

Subtraction Sandwiches

Solve the subtraction problems inside the sandwiches. Draw a line to match the problems that have the same difference.

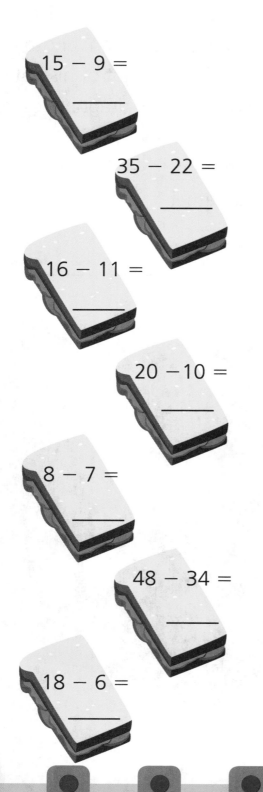

15 − 9 =

35 − 22 =

16 − 11 =

20 − 10 =

8 − 7 =

48 − 34 =

18 − 6 =

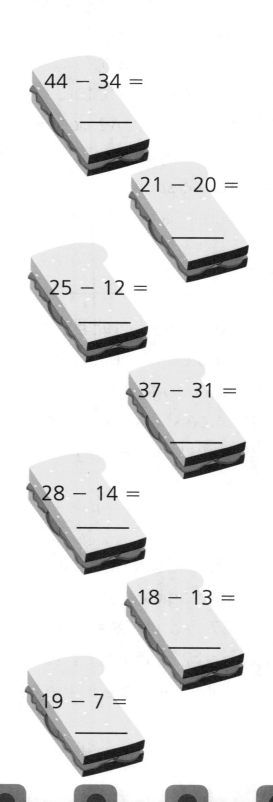

44 − 34 =

21 − 20 =

25 − 12 =

37 − 31 =

28 − 14 =

18 − 13 =

19 − 7 =

Time to Take Off!

Subtract to solve each problem.

1. 43
− 31

2. 57
− 44

25
− 13
12

3. 68
− 36

4. 279
− 36

5. 650
− 40

6. 366
− 43

7. 650
− 420

8. 803
− 802

9. 655
− 512

10. 438
− 215

11. 507
− 100

12. 794
− 431

Take Away Tables

Take away the value at the top of the table from each number on the left. Write the difference on the right. Complete all ten tables on both pages.

− 3	
8	
4	
6	
10	
9	

− 1	
7	
11	
2	
4	
1	

− 7	
9	
10	
14	
8	
13	

− 9	
18	
15	
11	
13	
17	

− 0	
10	
3	
1	
12	
2	

− 4	
5	
8	
10	
4	
7	

− 6	
12	
14	
7	
10	
9	

− 2	
5	
3	
9	
7	
4	

− 8	
10	
15	
9	
16	
11	

− 5	
9	
15	
12	
8	
10	

Regrouping Rocket Race

Subtract to solve each problem, and remember to regroup and rename. Then compare the two answers. Write **<**, **>**, or **=** in each circle. Count the number of times each symbol appears and write the totals on the rockets below. The rocket with the highest number wins the race! The first one is done for you.

1.
$$\begin{array}{r} \overset{3\ 13}{\cancel{43}} \\ -\ 26 \\ \hline 17 \end{array}$$
$$\bigcirc >$$
$$\begin{array}{r} \overset{4\ 10}{\cancel{50}} \\ -\ 35 \\ \hline 15 \end{array}$$

2.
$$\begin{array}{r} 23 \\ -\ 15 \\ \hline \end{array}$$
$$\bigcirc$$
$$\begin{array}{r} 31 \\ -\ 12 \\ \hline \end{array}$$

3.
$$\begin{array}{r} 46 \\ -\ 19 \\ \hline \end{array}$$
$$\bigcirc$$
$$\begin{array}{r} 41 \\ -14 \\ \hline \end{array}$$

4.
$$\begin{array}{r} 55 \\ -\ 27 \\ \hline \end{array}$$
$$\bigcirc$$
$$\begin{array}{r} 61 \\ -\ 33 \\ \hline \end{array}$$

5.
$$\begin{array}{r} 77 \\ -\ 29 \\ \hline \end{array}$$
$$\bigcirc$$
$$\begin{array}{r} 65 \\ -\ 16 \\ \hline \end{array}$$

6.
$$\begin{array}{r} 72 \\ -\ 55 \\ \hline \end{array}$$
$$\bigcirc$$
$$\begin{array}{r} 50 \\ -\ 33 \\ \hline \end{array}$$

Submarine Subtraction

Subtract to solve the problems. Remember to regroup and rename.

1. 461
  − 43

2. 130
  − 26

$$\begin{array}{r} \overset{13}{1\,\overset{13}{\cancel{3}}\,\overset{13}{\cancel{3}}} \\ \cancel{243} \\ -55 \\ \hline 188 \end{array}$$

3. 108
  − 54

4. 756
  − 69

5. 525
  − 47

6. 303
  − 25

7. 870
  − 561

8. 532
  − 250

9. 182
  − 103

10. 215
  − 127

11. 906
  − 417

12. 774
  − 597

Sporty Subtraction

Solve each subtraction problem. Write the answer in the sentence to complete the fun fact about each sport.

1.

$$\begin{array}{r} 1982 \\ -52 \\ \hline \end{array}$$

The first World Cup soccer game was played in the year _____.

2.

$$\begin{array}{r} 393 \\ -138 \\ \hline \end{array}$$

A volleyball weighs about _____ grams.

3.

$$\begin{array}{r} 465 \\ -365 \\ \hline \end{array}$$

A football field is _____ yards long.

4.

$$\begin{array}{r} 927 \\ -627 \\ \hline \end{array}$$

A perfect score in bowling is _____ points.

5.

$$\begin{array}{r} 490 \\ -418 \\ \hline \end{array}$$

Each baseball game begins with _____ new baseballs.

6.

$$\begin{array}{r} 184 \\ -168 \\ \hline \end{array}$$

The ice for a hockey game is kept at _____ degrees Fahrenheit.

Minus Linus

Solve the problems.

1. Linus had a collection of 356 stickers. He gave 48 stickers to his brother. Then he gave 36 more to his sister. How many stickers does he have left?

_____

2. On Saturday, Linus built a tower using 247 blocks. On Sunday, he used 306 blocks to build a tower. How many more blocks did he use on Sunday?

_____

3. Linus had a notebook with 400 sheets of blank paper. During the week he used 12 sheets of paper for math work. He also used 9 sheets of paper for spelling practice. How many blank sheets of paper does he have left?

_____

4. Linus ate 56 jellybeans this week. He also gave 18 jellybeans to his sister. If he started out with 312 jellybeans, how many does he have left?

_____

Fishy Fact Families

Use the numbers inside the fishes to fill in the equations in each tank. Complete all the fact families on both pages. The first one is done for you.

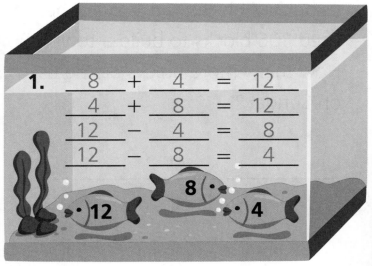

1.

$8 + 4 = 12$

$4 + 8 = 12$

$12 - 4 = 8$

$12 - 8 = 4$

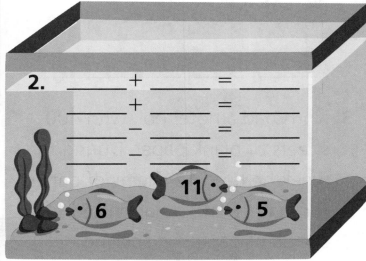

2.

____ + ____ = ____

____ + ____ = ____

____ − ____ = ____

____ − ____ = ____

3.

____ + ____ = ____

____ + ____ = ____

____ − ____ = ____

____ − ____ = ____

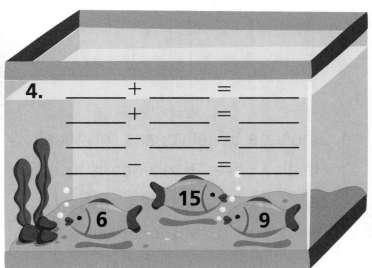

4.

____ + ____ = ____

____ + ____ = ____

____ − ____ = ____

____ − ____ = ____

5. _____ + _____ = _____
   _____ + _____ = _____
   _____ − _____ = _____
   _____ − _____ = _____

6. _____ + _____ = _____
   _____ + _____ = _____
   _____ − _____ = _____
   _____ − _____ = _____

7. _____ + _____ = _____
   _____ + _____ = _____
   _____ − _____ = _____
   _____ − _____ = _____

8. _____ + _____ = _____
   _____ + _____ = _____
   _____ − _____ = _____
   _____ − _____ = _____

The Greater Skater

Add or subtract to solve each problem, and remember to regroup and rename. Compare the two answers. Write **<**, **>**, or **=** in each circle. Count the number of times each symbol appears and write the total on the skateboards below. The skateboard with the highest number wins the competition!

1. 32   ◯   95
   + 69   − 26

2. 354   ◯   510
   + 67   − 62

3. 91   ◯   58
   − 32   + 42

4. 103   ◯   31
   − 38   + 12

5. 565   ◯   183
   − 276   + 106

6. 129   ◯   460
   − 59   − 261

Let's Recycle

Solve the problems.

1. The first-graders collected 235 bottles to recycle. The second-graders collected 188 bottles, and the third-graders collected 212 bottles. How many bottles did all three grades collect?

_____

3. Clover School had a recycling drive. The lower grades collected 332 cans and 444 bottles. The upper grades collected 303 cans and 358 bottles. How many more bottles than cans did the whole school collect?

_____

4. Kate wanted to save 250 empty boxes to donate to the school for art projects. She saved 76 cereal boxes, 55 shoeboxes, and 101 tissue boxes. How many more boxes does she need to save to meet her goal?

_____

2. Josh and Zack had a contest to see who could collect more newspapers. Josh got 138 newspapers from his neighborhood and 45 newspapers from his classmates. Zack gathered 116 newspapers from his swim team and 104 from his Boy Scout troop. Which boy collected more newspapers, and how many more did he collect?

_____

Camp Caravan

The graph shows how many kids were at Camp Caravan each month.
Use the graph to answer the questions below.

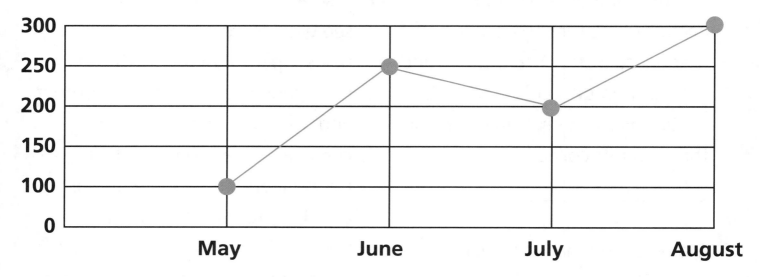

1. How many kids were at Camp Caravan in June, July, and August altogether?_____

2. How many more campers were there in August compared to May?_____

3. Between June and July, did the number of campers increase or decrease?

   _____

4. Were there more campers in May and June combined, or in July and August combined? _____

5. Which two months added together had a total of 450 campers?

   _____ _____

Bake Sale

Mr. Wang's class had a bake sale to raise money. The students sold cookies, lemon bars, brownies, cupcakes, and tarts. The graph shows how many of each item were sold at the bake sale. Use the information in the box to label the left side of the graph with the baked items.

They sold the same number of cookies as brownies.

Fifteen more cupcakes were sold than lemon bars.

The total number of cookies and tarts sold equals 40.

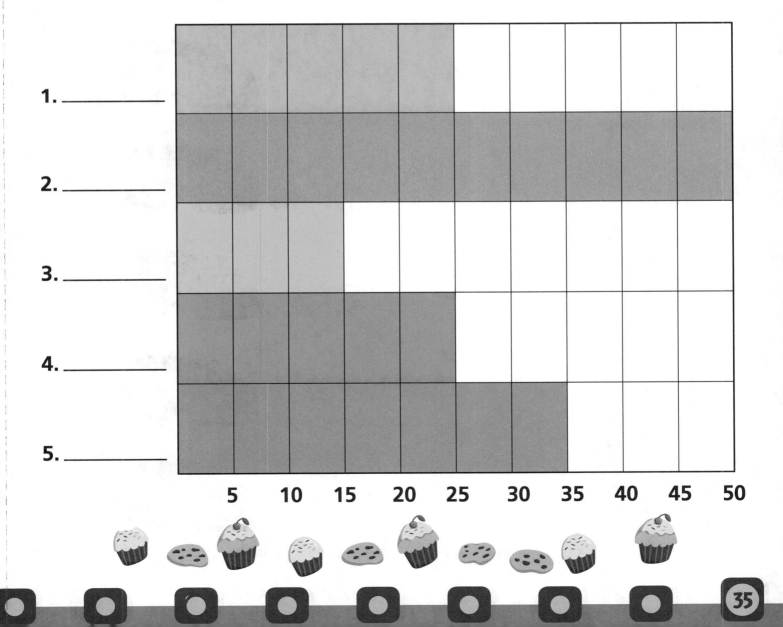

1. _____

2. _____

3. _____

4. _____

5. _____

5   10   15   20   25   30   35   40   45   50

Multiplication Mates

Multiply to solve the problems inside the socks and shoes. Draw a line to match each sock with the shoe that has the same product.

 2 × 2 = _____

 9 × 4 = _____

3 × 4 = _____

 2 × 9 = _____

6 × 6 = _____

 6 × 5 = _____

5 × 4 = _____

1 × 4 = _____

6 × 3 = _____

 6 × 2 = _____

4 × 4 = _____

 10 × 2 = _____

10 × 3 = _____

 8 × 2 = _____

True or False?

Read each problem carefully and decide whether it is a true math sentence.
Circle *True* or *False*.

1. $4 \times 0 = 0$

True   False

2. $3 \times 6 = 6 \times 3$

True   False

3. $10 \times 0 = 10$

True   False

4. $2 \times 4 \times 2 = 4 \times 2 \times 4$

True   False

5. $3 \times 0 = 5 \times 0$

True   False

6. $5 \times 1 = 5$

True   False

7. $1 \times 0 = 1$

True   False

8. $4 \times 3 \times 5 = 5 \times 3 \times 4$

True   False

9. $3 \times 7 = 7 \times 3$

True   False

10. $5 \times 1 = 1 + 5$

True   False

11. $1 \times 1 = 1$

True   False

12. $(6 \times 3) \times 2 = (6 \times 2) \times 3$

True   False

Times Tables

Multiply each number by the value on the far left. Write the product on the bottom row. Complete all the tables on both pages. The first problem is done for you.

	0	1	2	3	4	5	6	7	8	9	10
× 2	0										

	0	1	2	3	4	5	6	7	8	9	10
× 3											

	0	1	2	3	4	5	6	7	8	9	10
× 4											

	0	1	2	3	4	5	6	7	8	9	10
5											

× 6	0	1	2	3	4	5	6	7	8	9	10

× 7	0	1	2	3	4	5	6	7	8	9	10

× 8	0	1	2	3	4	5	6	7	8	9	10

× 9	0	1	2	3	4	5	6	7	8	9	10

× 10	0	1	2	3	4	5	6	7	8	9	10

Time Flies

Multiply to solve each problem and compare the two products. Write **<**, **>**, or **=** in each circle. Count the number of times each symbol appears and write the totals on the airplanes below. The airplane with the highest number wins the race!

1. 12 ○ 10
    × 4   × 5

2. 11 ○ 12
    × 5   × 3

3. 10 ○ 20
    × 4   × 2

4. 14 ○ 13
    × 2   × 3

5. 12 ○ 11
    × 2   × 3

6. 13 ○ 10
    × 2   × 3

Multiplication Masterpiece

Multiply and regroup to solve the problems.

1. 16
$\times$ 4

2. 32
$\times$ 8

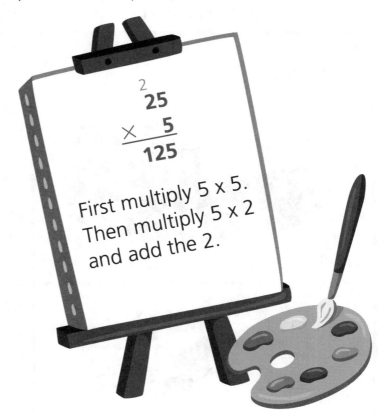

First multiply 5 x 5.
Then multiply 5 x 2
and add the 2.

3. 63
$\times$ 4

4. 81
$\times$ 2

5. 59
$\times$ 3

6. 73
$\times$ 2

7. 52
$\times$ 2

8. 27
$\times$ 6

9. 70
$\times$ 7

10. 66
$\times$ 8

11. 43
$\times$ 9

12. 98
$\times$ 4

From Time to Time

Multiply and regroup to solve each problem.
Write the product on the line to show the year for each event.

1.

$$119 \times 4$$

_____

The Roman Empire ended.

2.

$$746 \times 2$$

_____

Columbus set sail.

3.

$$111 \times 16$$

_____

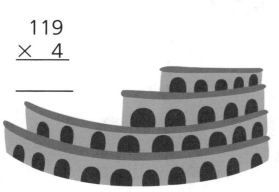

The Declaration of
Independence was signed.

4.

$$97 \times 8$$

_____ BCE

The first Olympic games were held
in ancient Greece.

5.

$$23 \times 81$$

_____

Abraham Lincoln
gave the
Gettysburg Address.

6.

$$179 \times 11$$

_____

Neil Armstrong walked on the
moon.

Multiplication Vacation

Solve the problems.

1. The airplane flying to Hawaii had 22 rows of seats. There were 9 seats in each row. How many total seats were on the plane?

_____

2. The tour company had 15 boats for snorkeling. Each boat could hold 8 people. Every day, each boat went out on 2 snorkel trips. How many people could go on the snorkel tour each day?

_____

3. The Madsen family went on a hiking vacation. For the first 3 days, they hiked 5 miles each day. On the last 2 days, they hiked 3 miles a day. How many miles did they hike altogether on the trip?

_____

4. On the first day of Vince's fishing trip, he caught 4 fish each hour. On the second day, Vince caught 2 fish an hour. Vince fished for 5 hours on both days of his trip. How many fish did he catch altogether?

_____

Division Dogs

Divide to solve the problems inside the dog bones and collars.
Draw a line to match each bone with the collar that has the same quotient.

$16 \div 4 =$ _____

$15 \div 3 =$ _____

$24 \div 4 =$ _____

$45 \div 5 =$ _____

$56 \div 8 =$ _____

$21 \div 7 =$ _____

$64 \div 8 =$ _____

$16 \div 2 =$ _____

$27 \div 3 =$ _____

$32 \div 8 =$ _____

$42 \div 6 =$ _____

$36 \div 6 =$ _____

$6 \div 2 =$ _____

$20 \div 4 =$ _____

Truth Sleuth

Read each problem carefully and decide whether it is a true math sentence.
Circle *True* or *False*.

1. $7 \div 0 = 0$

True   False

2. $10 \div 1 = 1$

True   False

3. $15 \div 5 = 5 \div 15$

True   False

4. $5 \div 1 = 5$

True   False

5. $(24 \div 6) \div 2 = 24 \div (6 \div 2)$

True   False

6. $12 \div 12 = 1$

True   False

7. $3 \div 0 = 0$

True   False

8. $4 \div 1 = 4 \div 1$

True   False

9. $0 \div 9 = 9$

True   False

10. $10 \div 0 = 0 \div 10$

True   False

11. $1 \div 0 = 1$

True   False

12. $0 \div 5 = 0$

True   False

Division Tables

Divide each number by the value on the far left. Write the answer on the bottom row. Complete all the tables on both pages. The first problem is done for you.

	14	8	12	18	16	10	6	4	2	20
÷ 2	7									

	18	27	30	9	21	15	12	24	6	3
÷ 3										

	20	36	8	12	24	16	28	4	32	40
÷ 4										

	10	50	35	20	15	45	25	40	30	5
÷ 5										

	18	24	36	54	42	30	48	60	6	12
÷ 6										

	49	70	21	35	63	14	7	42	28	56
÷ 7										

	80	40	64	16	72	8	32	56	24	48
÷ 8										

	72	27	54	18	63	36	90	81	9	45
÷ 9										

	30	40	60	100	50	80	20	10	90	70
÷10										

The Long Way Home

Use long division to solve each problem. If the quotient is an even number, color the circle. See what path the kids took to get home.

8)112

5)215

9)162

7)385

12)144

6)132

4)144

6)126

3)57

9)117

11)220

4)120

3)78

Dive Into Division

Use long division to solve the problems. The answers will have remainders.

1. 5)223

2. 7)732

$$
\begin{array}{r}
153 \text{ R1} \\
3\overline{)460} \\
-3 \\
\hline
16 \\
-15 \\
\hline
10 \\
-9 \\
\hline
1
\end{array}
$$

3. 4)938

4. 2)505

5. 9)106

6. 3)695

7. 6)206

8. 8)589

9. 12)169

10. 6)223

11. 10)358

12. 11)456

Record Remainder

Use long division to solve each problem. Each answer will have a remainder. Look at the bottom of the page and find the quotient. Write the remainder for that quotient on the line above. The first one is done for you.

1.
```
    75 R2
4)302
  −28
   22
  −20
    2
```

2. 5)869

3. 11)152

4. 6)560

5. 6)229

6. 8)203

In ____00____, kids from all over the world gathered to make the world's
    93   173

longest line of footprints. There were ____0,____ ____ __2__ footprints in
                    38   13   25 75

the line.

Dinnertime Division

Solve the problems.

1. Grace is planning to feed 8 people for dinner. She has 256 peas. If she wants to give each person the same number of peas, how many peas should she put on each plate? _____

2. Morgan needs to fill 12 cups with ice for the dinner party. He has 74 ice cubes. If he uses as many cubes as he can and puts an equal number in each cup, how many ice cubes will be left over?

_____

3. Mr. Lee made 150 dinner rolls for the banquet. Each breadbasket can hold 8 dinner rolls. How many breadbaskets will Mr. Lee need to hold all of his rolls? _____

4. Kate wanted to put cherries on everyone's ice cream sundaes after dinner. She had 45 cherries to use. She put 5 cherries on each sundae. How many sundaes were there? _____

Family Flag Match

Complete the equations in each flag. Then draw a line to connect the flags whose problems are in the same family.

$4 \times 3 =$ _____
$3 \times$ _____ $= 12$

$2 \times$ _____ $= 10$
$5 \times 2 =$ _____

$32 \div 4 =$ _____
_____ $\div 8 = 4$

_____ $\div 2 = 7$
$14 \div 7 =$ _____

_____ $\times 2 = 14$
$2 \times 7 =$ _____

_____ $\times 8 = 32$
$8 \times 4 =$ _____

$10 \div$ _____ $= 5$
$10 \div$ _____ $= 2$

$3 \times 9 =$ _____
$9 \times$ _____ $= 27$

_____ $\div 3 = 9$
$27 \div$ _____ $= 3$

$12 \div$ _____ $= 4$
_____ $\div 4 = 3$

Practice Makes Perfect

Practice your multiplication and division. Don't forget to regroup or use long division as you solve the problems.

1. 35
 × 5

2. 6)624

3. 244
 × 3

4. 8)186

5. 3)517

6. 23
 × 14

7. 30
 × 61

8. 4)906

9. 105
 × 4

10. 10)350

11. 217
 × 30

12. 7)253

Go Team!

Fill in × or ÷ to make each math sentence true. Count the number of times each sign appears and write the total on the scoreboard below. See which team won the game!

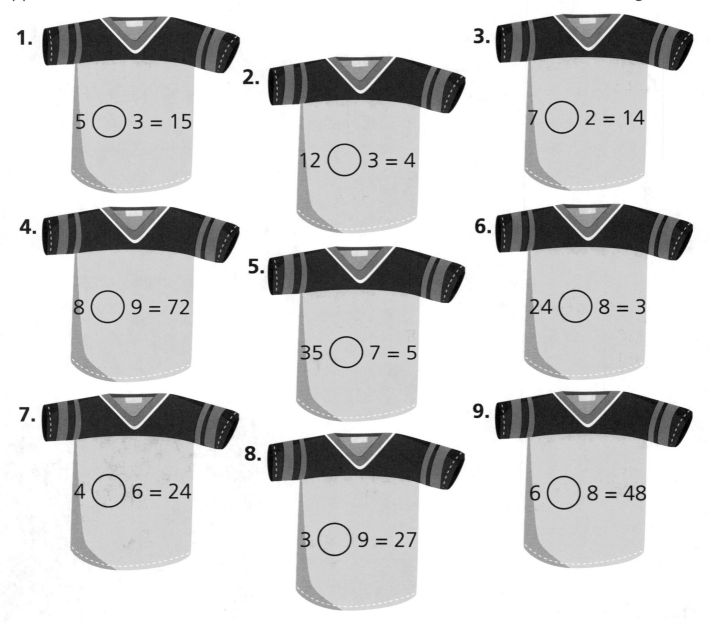

1. 5 ◯ 3 = 15

2. 12 ◯ 3 = 4

3. 7 ◯ 2 = 14

4. 8 ◯ 9 = 72

5. 35 ◯ 7 = 5

6. 24 ◯ 8 = 3

7. 4 ◯ 6 = 24

8. 3 ◯ 9 = 27

9. 6 ◯ 8 = 48

scoreboard

× = ◯   ÷ = ◯

Soccer Stories

Solve the problems.

1. The children on the soccer team practiced 3 days a week. They practiced for 16 weeks before the big game. How many total days did they practice before the big game?

_____

2. There were 150 kids at the soccer camp. They needed to get into groups of 6 for the first soccer drill. How many groups were there?

_____

3. On the day of the soccer championship, 312 people will come to he game. The field has bleachers where people can sit to watch the game. There is room for a maximum of 25 people on each bleacher. How many rows of bleachers will be needed to fit all the people?

_____

4. The members of the soccer team sold raffle tickets to raise money for their uniforms. Each player sold 32 tickets. There were 18 kids on the team. How many tickets did the team sell altogether?

_____

Speedy Readers

Five kids kept track of how many library books they read each week. As soon as they had read five books, they got to put a book sticker on the chart. They kept track for two weeks. Use the chart to answer the questions below.

	Week 1	**Week 2**
Ruby	📕 📕 📕	📕
Jack	📕 📕	📕 📕
Natalie	📕 📕 📕	📕 📕
Ben	📕	📕 📕 📕
Ashley	📕 📕 📕 📕	📕 📕 📕

Each 📕 = 5 books

1. Which two students read 15 books each during Week 1?

_____ _____

2. How many books did Ashley read during Week 1? _____

3. How many total books did Ben read during Weeks 1 and 2?

_____

4. Which student read 10 books each week? _____

5. Which student read the most books during the two weeks?

_____

Sticker Store

The chart shows how many of each type of sticker the store has in stock. Use the chart to answer the questions below.

 🦋	 ❤️	 🙂	 ⭐
96	80	216	100

1. There are 8 kids who want to buy butterfly stickers. How many can each child buy if all 8 want to have the same number of butterfly stickers?

_____

2. Ten kids came into the sticker store. They each bought 10 of the same kind of sticker. They bought all the stickers the store had in stock for that shape. Which type of sticker did they buy? _____

3. Helen bought all the smiley face stickers in the store to put in her party favor bags. She wants to fill 8 party favor bags with an equal number of stickers. How many smiley face stickers can she put in each bag?

_____

4. Three kids bought all the heart stickers in the store. They divided them into 3 equal groups, but there were a few left over. How many stickers were left over? _____

5. Ms. Norris wanted to buy stickers for her class. She bought all the butterfly and heart stickers the store had in stock. After she divided them into equal groups, each student got 8 stickers. How many students are in her class? _____

Fraction Match

How much of each figure is shaded? Draw a line to the correct fraction.

1.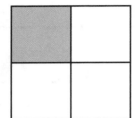

2.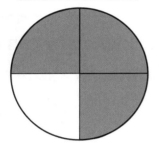

3.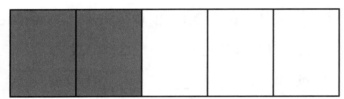

4.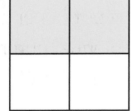

5.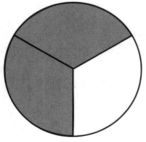

6.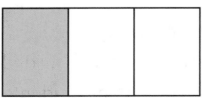

$\frac{2}{5}$

$\frac{1}{3}$

$\frac{2}{3}$

$\frac{1}{4}$

$\frac{1}{2}$

$\frac{3}{4}$

Made in the Shade

Write a fraction to show how much of each figure is shaded.

1.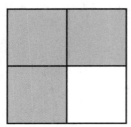

_____

2.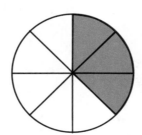

_____

3.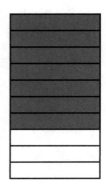

_____

4.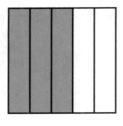

_____

5.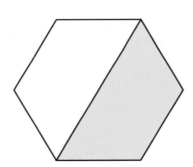

_____

6.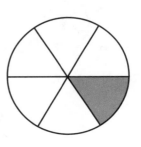

_____

Shade the correct number of parts on each picture so it matches the fraction.

7. $\dfrac{2}{3}$

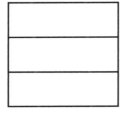

8. $\dfrac{1}{4}$

9. $\dfrac{2}{5}$

Pizza Party

Write a fraction to show how many slices are left in each pizza. Compare the two fractions and pictures and fill in the **<**, **>**, or **=** symbol. The first one is done for you.

1.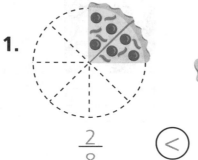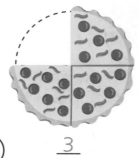

$\frac{2}{8}$ ⬤< $\frac{3}{4}$

2.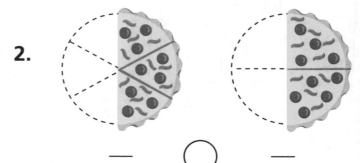

— ◯ —

3.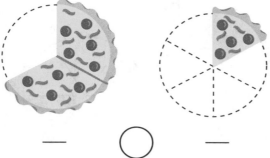

— ◯ —

4.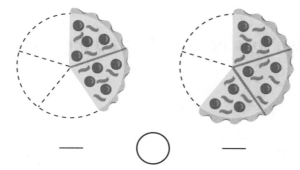

— ◯ —

5.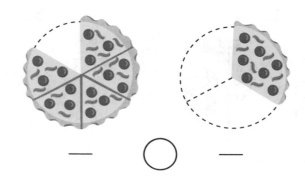

— ◯ —

6.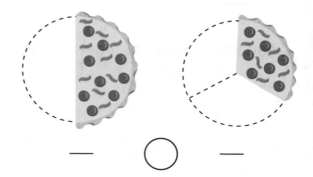

— ◯ —

Frosty Fractions

Add or subtract the fractions.

1. $\dfrac{3}{4} - \dfrac{1}{4} = \underline{\quad}$

2. $\dfrac{1}{3} + \dfrac{1}{3} = \underline{\quad}$

3. $\dfrac{4}{5} - \dfrac{2}{5} = \underline{\quad}$

4. $\dfrac{3}{8} + \dfrac{2}{8} = \underline{\quad}$

5. $\dfrac{7}{10} - \dfrac{3}{10} = \underline{\quad}$

6. $\dfrac{1}{7} + \dfrac{3}{7} = \underline{\quad}$

7. $\dfrac{1}{6} + \dfrac{4}{6} = \underline{\quad}$

8. $\dfrac{3}{9} + \dfrac{2}{9} = \underline{\quad}$

9. $\dfrac{6}{7} - \dfrac{1}{7} = \underline{\quad}$

10. $\dfrac{7}{8} - \dfrac{1}{8} = \underline{\quad}$

11. $\dfrac{2}{10} + \dfrac{7}{10} = \underline{\quad}$

12. $\dfrac{5}{9} - \dfrac{3}{9} = \underline{\quad}$

A-MAZE-ing Fractions

Start in the middle of the maze and find your way to each exit. All the fractions along the correct trail are equivalent. Look in the box at the bottom to find the lowest terms fraction for the equivalent fractions on each trail.
Write it at the maze exit.

$\dfrac{1}{2}$

$\dfrac{1}{3}$ $\dfrac{1}{4}$ $\dfrac{1}{2}$ $\dfrac{2}{3}$

Dreamy Decimals

Add or subtract the decimals.

1. $5.50
    + $2.75
   (handwritten: 1)
   (handwritten: $8.25)

2. $6.04
    − $5.30
   (handwritten: 5 10)
   (handwritten: $0.74)

(thought bubble:)
```
        4 12              1
     $3.52           $4.35
   − $2.25         + $3.26
      1.27            7.61
```
Bring the decimal down.

3. $25.50
    − $18.25
   (handwritten: 1 15 4 10)
   (handwritten: 07.25)

4. $4.80
    + $3.08
   (handwritten: 7 10)
   (handwritten: $1.72)

5. $12.04
    − $5.30
   (handwritten: 0 11 10)
   (handwritten: $06.74)

6. $35.12
    − $30.50
   (handwritten: 4 11)
   (handwritten: $04.62)

7. $5.24
    + $2.02
   (handwritten: $7.26)

8. $112.20
    + $15.85
   (handwritten: 1)
   (handwritten: $128.05)

9. $9.45
    − $ .32
   (handwritten: $9.13)

10. $6.03
    + $ .98
   (handwritten: 5 10 13 9)
   (handwritten: $5.05)

11. $220.50
    + $ .95
   (handwritten: 9 14 10)
   (handwritten: 219.55)

12. $150.00
    − $75.50
   (handwritten: 14 9 0 4 10 0)
   (handwritten: $074.50)

The Price Is Right

Multiply or divide to solve each problem. Write each answer in the sentence to find out how much each item cost.

1.   3.02
        × 5

The Brooklyn Bridge cost _____ million dollars to build in 1883.

2. 30)1.5

In 1903, the first box of crayons sold for $ _____.

3.   .75
        × 2

In 1917, the first pair of sneakers cost $_____.

4.   49.5
        × 2

In 1904, you could buy a Model T car for $_____.

5. 24).24

The first postage stamp was sold in Great Britain for $_____.

6. 65)1.3

You could buy a chocolate bar for $_____ in 1900.

What's the Change?

Solve the problems.

1. Sarah bought 5 pencils and 2 notebooks. The pencils cost 25 cents each and the notebooks cost $1.50 each. She paid with a five-dollar bill. How much change did she get back?

_____

2. David wanted to buy a new eraser for each person in his math study group. Erasers cost 35 cents each. There are 12 kids in his math study group. He paid with four $1 bills and one quarter. How much change did he get back?

_____

3. Lisa wanted to get a folder for each subject in school. She needed one each for reading, math, science, and social studies. Each folder cost $2.50. She paid with one bill, and she didn't get any change back. What type of bill did she pay with?

_____

4. Monique needed to get supplies for art class. Markers cost $2.50 and colored pencils cost $3.00. She bought one set of markers and pencils for herself, and one for her friend. She paid with a twenty-dollar bill. How much change did she get back?

_____

Apples and Oranges

Fractions and decimals look different, but they are just two ways of showing the same amount. Draw a line to match the amounts that are equal.

50 cents

.1

30 seconds

$ 0.25

.9

$ 0.75

$\frac{9}{10}$

$\frac{3}{4}$ of a dollar

$\frac{1}{10}$

$\frac{1}{2}$ of a dollar

$\frac{1}{4}$ of a dollar

$\frac{1}{2}$ of a minute

Mix It Up!

Add, subtract, multiply, or divide to solve the problems.

1. $4.65
       + $3.45

2. 6)$1.50

3. $5.25
      ×   8

4. $8.25
       − $4.50

5. 6)$.48

6. $12.80
       − $10.05

7. $2.13
       + $3.88

8. $3.55
      ×   4

9. 3)$2.55

10. $1.99
       ×   3

11. $20.00
        − $ 8.79

12. $4.99
        + $1.69

Fraction Favorites

The school newspaper took a poll of the students' favorite candies. The circle graph shows what fraction of the students voted for each type of candy. Use the circle graph to answer the questions below.

1. Which two candies each got $\frac{1}{3}$ of the students' votes?

_____ _____

2. What fraction of the students voted for lollipops as their favorite?

_____

3. If you combine the votes for lemon drops and for bubble gum, what is the total fraction? _____

4. What fraction of the students voted for bubble gum, lemon drops, and chocolate bars altogether? _____

5. Which two candies each received one-sixth of the vote?

_____ _____

Decimal Diner

Use the menu to answer the questions below.

Menu

Hot Dog	$ 1.25	Fries	Small	$ .85
Pizza	$ 1.75		Large	$ 1.65
		Soda		$ 1.10
Hamburger	$ 2.15	Juice		$ 1.30
Chicken	$ 2.60	Milk		$ .95

1. Nikki ordered a hamburger, large fries, and a soda. She paid with a five-dollar bill. How much was her change?_____

2. The 8 kids in the chess club went out to eat after the chess match. They each ordered a soda. Half of them ordered small fries and the other half ordered large fries. How much did their food cost in all?

_____

3. Five friends went to the diner for a snack. They decided to split the chicken and large fries. They shared the cost equally. How much did each person need to pay? _____

4. Jason had pizza and milk for lunch. Mary bought a hot dog, small fries, and a juice. How much more did Mary spend for her lunch?

_____

5. Becca wants to buy chicken, small fries, and a soda. She has four dollar bills and two quarters. How much more money does she need?

_____

Ship Shapes

Match each picture or phrase with the ship that gives the shape's name.

a six-sided shape

a shape with eight sides

octagon

pentagon

cube

pyramid

hexagon

trapezoid

triangular prism

Perimeter Pairs

Calculate the perimeter of each figure. Compare the perimeters of both figures and fill in the **<**, **>**, or **=** symbol. The first one is done for you.

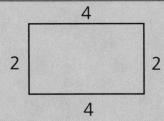

$$4 + 2 + 4 + 2 = 12 \text{ inches}$$

The perimeter is the distance around a figure. Add all the sides together.

1.

4
4 □ 4
4

5
3 ▭ 3
5

__16__ inches (**=**) __16__ inches

2.

5
4 ▭ 4
5

3
3 ⬡ 3
3   3
3

____ feet ( ) ____ feet

3.

4 △ 4
3

2
2 □ 2
2

____ inches (<) ____ inches

4.

3
3 □ 3
3

6 △ 6
2

____ feet ( ) ____ feet

5.

4 ⬠ 4
4   4
4

8
2 ▭ 2
8

____ inches ( ) ____ inches

6.

2
2 ⬡ 2
2   2
2

6 △ 6
3

____ feet ( ) ____ feet

71

Figure It Out!

Calculate the area or the volume of each figure.

4 inches

2 inches

Area = length × width
4 × 2 = 8 inches²

2 inches

1 inch

2 inches

Volume = length × width × height
2 × 1 × 2 = 4 inches³

1.

3 feet

2 feet

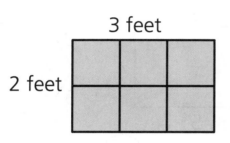

Area = _____ feet²

2.

5 feet

3 feet

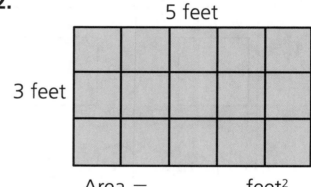

Area = _____ feet²

3.

3 feet

1 foot

2 feet

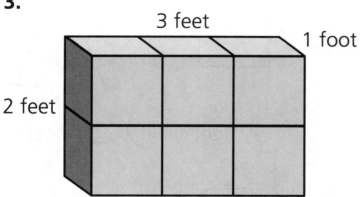

Area = _____ feet³

4.

2 feet

3 feet

2 feet

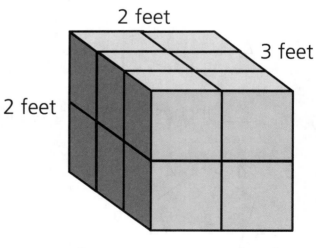

Area = _____ feet³

How Does Your Garden Grow?

Solve the problems.

1. Lucy's garden patch is a rectangular shape. It measures 8 feet long and 4 feet wide. If Lucy walks around the perimeter of her garden patch, what would the total distance be?

_____

2. Diego wants to figure out how many square feet of soil he needs to cover his garden patch. He has a square-shaped patch that measures 5 feet on each side. How many square feet of soil does he need?

_____

3. Kayla and Trina both have small garden patches. Each one is 3 feet long and 2 feet wide. They need at least 10 square feet to grow pumpkins. If they combine their patches, will they have enough space?

_____

4. Carl has built a special gardening bed so he can have deep soil. The bed is 6 feet long, 3 feet wide, and 2 feet deep. What is the total volume of the gardening bed?

_____

Triangle Types

Write the word that describes each triangle.

Equilateral

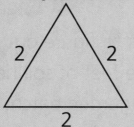

All 3 sides are equal

Isosceles

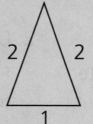

2 sides are equal

Right

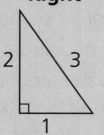

90 degree angle

1.

_____

2.

_____

3.

_____

4.

_____

5.

_____

6.

_____

7.

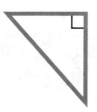

_____

8.

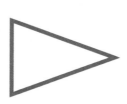

_____

9.

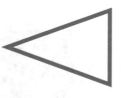

_____

The Right Way

Rick needs to find the right way home.
Follow the trail of triangles with right angles to find his house. Then circle it.

Hint:
A right triangle has one L-shaped angle that equals 90 degrees.

Estimate It!

Find the word that makes the best estimate for each item and write it on the line.

ounces	centimeters	ruler	tons	grams
inches	pounds	feet	scale	

1.

A penny weighs 3 _____.

2.

A school bus weighs 15 _____.

3.

A bee is 2 _____ long.

4.

A bowling ball weighs 9 _____.

5.

A juice box weighs 8 _____.

6.

To measure the width of a book, use a _____.

7.

A surfboard is 8 _____ long.

8.

A pencil is 7_____ long.

9.

To weigh a bag of apples, use a _____.

Measure for Measure

Read each problem and convert the measurement.

1. 2 hours = _____ minutes

2. 24 inches = _____ feet

3. 2 yards = _____ feet

4. 3 feet = _____ inches

5. 180 minutes = _____ hours

6. 2 meters = _____ centimeters

7. 36 inches = _____ yard

8. 300 centimeters = _____ meters

9. 4 hours = _____ minutes

10. 5 meters = _____ centimeters

11. 120 minutes = _____ hours

12. 9 feet = _____ yards

Piano Practice

Brian practiced piano each day this week. The clock on the left shows the time he started practicing. The time below the clock is how long he practiced. Draw a line to the clock on the right that shows what time he stopped.

Monday

30 minutes

Tuesday

35 minutes

Wednesday

45 minutes

Thursday

45 minutes

Party Time!

Solve the problems.

1. The cupcakes need to bake for 20 minutes. The party is going to start at 5:00. Tina wants to make sure the cupcakes finish baking 20 minutes before the party starts. What time should she put the cupcakes into the oven?

_____

2. Taylor got enough lace to put around the border of a square tablecloth. The lace is 16 feet long. What is the length and width of the tablecloth?

_____

3. The first party guest arrived at 5:05. After that, one guest arrived every 5 minutes. There were 8 total party guests. What time did the final guest arrive?

_____

4. Taylor and Tina want to have 2 feet of ribbon tied to each balloon. They have 6 balloons. Each spool has 72 inches of ribbon. How many spools of ribbon will they need for all 6 balloons?

_____

The Class Quilt

The class divided into four groups to make a quilt. Each group made a design with four quilt squares and then they put the whole quilt together. Use the diagram of the quilt to answer the questions below.

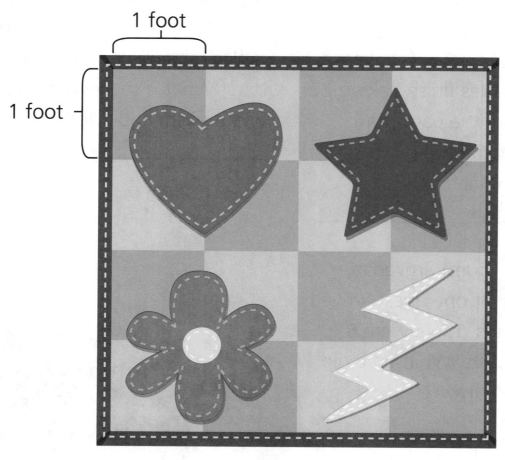

1 foot

1 foot

1. What is the area of the whole quilt? _____ feet^2

2. If they wanted to put ribbon around the perimeter of the quilt, how many feet of ribbon would they need? _____ feet

3. Find out the area of the quilt pieces that form the heart. _____ feet^2

4. What is the length of one side of the quilt in inches? _____

5. Find the perimeter of the quilt pieces that form the star. _____

Prime Times

Use the television program schedule to answer the questions below.

7:00 – 7:30	**Baking with Bonnie**
7:05 – 7:55	**Local News**
7:35 – 8:05	**Amy's Adventures**
7:55 – 8:50	**Fairytale Friends**
8:15 – 9:00	**The Spooky House**
8:30 – 9:30	**Animal Antics**

1. Which program lasts for 55 minutes? _____

2. Which two programs are the exact same length, and how long are they?

_____   _____

3. How much longer is Animal Antics than The Spooky House?

_____

4. Which show starts right after the Local News ends?

_____

5. If the clock shows this time, which programs are on?

_____

_____

_____

Catch Match

Read what's inside each bat. Draw a line to the equation or expression that means the same thing. The letter "*n*" stands for "a number."

4 plus a number equals 16.

$n \times 2 = 4 \times 6$

A number equals 16 minus 4.

$16 + n > 14$

2 times 6 is equal to 3 times a number.

$3 \times 6 = 2 \times n$

A number minus 6 is less than 3.

$4 + n = 16$

3 times 6 is equal to 2 times a number.

$16 - 4 = n$

6 plus a number is greater than 14.

$2 \times 6 = 3 \times n$

A number times 2 is equal to 4 times 6.

$n - 6 < 3$

Nuts About Numbers

Use the value for *n* at the top of each box to solve the equations.

n = 8

1. $4 + n =$ _____

2. $32 \div n =$ _____

3. $n - 6 =$ _____

n = 5

4. $n \times 3 =$ _____

5. $18 - n =$ _____

6. $n + n =$ _____

n = 4

7. $6 \times n =$ _____

8. $n + 12 =$ _____

9. $n \times n =$ _____

n = 10

10. $n \div 2 =$ _____

11. $17 - n =$ _____

12. $n + 12 =$ _____

Speedy Snowboarders

Each problem has a missing operation sign. Fill in the +, −, ×, or ÷ for each equation. Count the number of times each sign appears and write the total on the snowboards below. See which snowboard is the speediest!

1. 6 ◯ 5 = 11

2. 9 ◯ 4 = 36

3. 7 ◯ 8 = 15

4. 16 ◯ 9 = 7

5. 24 ◯ 3 = 8

6. 18 ◯ 9 = 2

7. 20 ◯ 12 = 8

8. 5 ◯ 6 = 30

9. 27 ◯ 9 = 3

10. 42 ◯ 7 = 6

+ ◯

× ◯

− ◯

÷ ◯

The Missing Number

Each equation has a missing number. Figure out what number makes the equation true and write it on the line.

1. $4 + \underline{\hspace{1cm}} = 16$

2. $\underline{\hspace{1cm}} \times 9 = 27$

3. $\underline{\hspace{1cm}} - 7 = 12$

4. $64 \div \underline{\hspace{1cm}} = 8$

5. $6 + \underline{\hspace{1cm}} + 3 = 13$

6. $3 \times 2 \times \underline{\hspace{1cm}} = 36$

7. $5 + \underline{\hspace{1cm}} = 7 + 3$

8. $6 \times 4 = 12 \times \underline{\hspace{1cm}}$

9. $16 - 6 = 2 \times \underline{\hspace{1cm}}$

10. $35 \div \underline{\hspace{1cm}} = 3 + 4$

11. $4 \times 5 = \underline{\hspace{1cm}} + 10$

12. $\underline{\hspace{1cm}} \div 7 = 9 - 6$

Puzzling Patterns

Start in the middle of the maze and find your way to each exit. The numbers along the correct trail to the exit follow a pattern. Figure out the rule for each pattern. What number would come next? Write the number in the box at the maze exit.

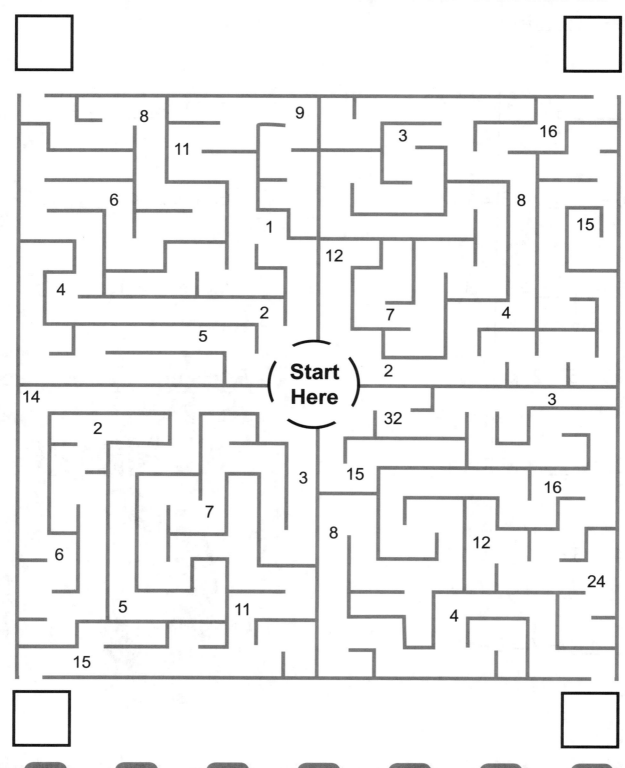

Solve that Sentence!

Read each problem carefully. Figure out what number makes the math sentence true and write it on the line.

1. If $9 \times 6 = 54$, then $6 \times 9 = $ _____

2. If $n = 12$, then $n \div 2 = $ _____

3. If each student needs 2 pencils, then a class of 15 students needs _____ total pencils.

4. If $n = 7$, then $5 \times n = $ _____

5. If $12 \times 8 = 96$, then $8 \times 12 = $ _____

6. If one box has 6 cookies, then 10 boxes have _____ cookies altogether.

7. If $4 \times 5 \times 2 = 40$, then $2 \times 4 \times 5 = $ _____

8. If $n = 3$, then $8 - n = $ _____

9. If $n = 6$, then $n + n = $ _____

10. If $2 \times 3 \times 8 = 48$, then $2 \times 8 \times 3 = $ _____

11. If one paperclip is 2 inches long, then 5 paperclips together are _____ inches long.

12. If $(5 \times 3) \times 2 = 30$, then $(2 \times 5) \times 3 = $ _____

The Busiest Burgerman

Which equation could you use to solve each problem?
Find the equation below and write it in the box.

1. The Burgerman made 40 French fries. He always puts 8 fries on each plate. Which number sentence shows how to find the number of plates he can serve?

2. Each bag of hamburger buns holds 40 buns. The Burgerman ordered 8. Which number sentence shows how to find the total number of buns in all the bags?

3. There are 8 pickles left in the jar. The Burgerman always puts 4 pickles on each burger. Which number sentence shows how to figure out the number of burgers he can put pickles on?

4. During lunch, 48 people ordered burgers. During dinner, 40 people ordered burgers. Which number sentence shows how many people ordered burgers during lunch and dinner?

5. The Burgerman has swiss, cheddar, American, and mozzarella cheese. He has 8 slices of each type of cheese. Which number sentence shows how many slices of cheese he has altogether?

6. The Burgerman filled a pitcher with 40 ice cubes. When he poured a drink, 8 cubes went into the glass. Which number sentence shows how many cubes are left in the pitcher?

$4 \times 8 =$ _____ $40 - 8 =$ _____ $40 \times 8 =$ _____

$48 + 40 =$ _____ $8 \div 4 =$ _____ $40 \div 8 =$ _____

School Supplies

Solve the problems.

1. Grace needs to buy a notebook with lined paper. One notebook has 70 sheets of paper and costs $1.40. The other notebook has 40 sheets of paper and costs $1.20. Which notebook should she buy to get the lowest price per sheet of paper?

_____

2. Mr. Douglas needs to buy 12 rulers for his classroom. If he orders them online, he can buy a package of 12 rulers for $6.00. If he goes to the store, he can buy each ruler for 40 cents. Where should he buy the rulers to spend the least amount of money?

_____

3. Max decided to make bookmarks and sell them to earn money. His mom spent $15.00 on the supplies to make the bookmarks. Max made 30 bookmarks and sold them for 75 cents each. How much money did he earn after he paid his mom back for the supplies?

_____

4. Ms. Lee needs to buy new backpacks for her two kids. One backpack costs $10.00. If you buy two backpacks, you get the second one for half off. How much did she pay for both backpacks?

_____

Goodie Bag

All of these toys are in the goodie bag at the doctor's office. Use the picture to figure out the probability for each question below. Circle the correct answer.

1. What are your chances of pulling a out of the goodie bag?

     a) 5 out of 5   b) 5 out of 12   c) 3 out of 12

2. What are your chances of getting a ?

     a) 1:4   b) 3:13   c) 4:12

3. Which fraction shows the odds of pulling out a ?

     a) $\dfrac{1}{2}$ b) $\dfrac{11}{12}$ c) $\dfrac{1}{12}$

4. What are the chances you will get a from the bag?

     a) 3 out of 4   b) 1 out of 3   c) 1 out of 4

5. What are your chances of pulling out either a or a ?

     a) 30%   b) 20%   c) 50%

Goodie Bag Graph

The doctor needs a graph showing all the toys she has in her goodie bag.
Use the picture on page 90 to complete the graph. Make a bar to show how many of each toy are in the bag.

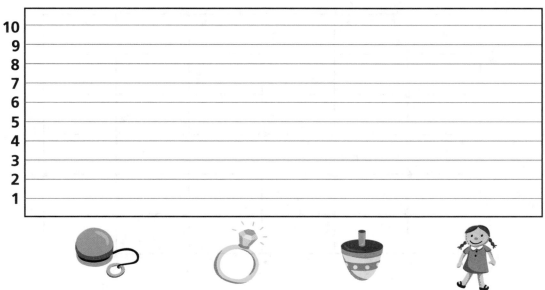

Use the graph to answer the questions.

1. Two kids came to the doctor's office and they each pulled out a yo-yo. How many toys are left in the goodie bag now? _____

2. The doctor added 4 toy rings, 4 dolls, and 1 yo-yo to the goodie bag. Which toy has the greatest number in the goodie bag now?

   _____

3. Jack pulled a ring out of the bag and Laura pulled out a yo-yo. How many yo-yos are left in the goodie bag now? _____

4. At the end of the day, 4 yo-yos and 1 top had been pulled out of the bag. All the other toys were still in the bag. Which two toys had the same number in the bag at the end of the day? _____

Graph and Laugh

Find each ordered pair on the graph. Remember, the first number tells how many spaces you move to the right, and the second number tells how many spaces up. Then write the letter you found at each point on the line above the pair.

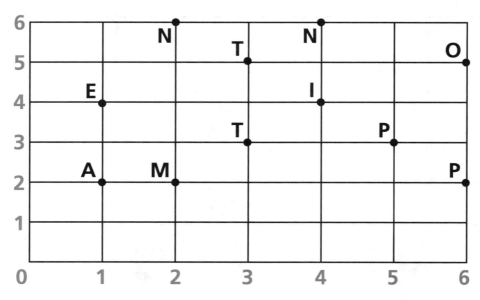

Why was the student rushing to find all the ordered pairs?

He was late for an

 A ___ - ___ ___ ___ ___ ___ - ___ ___ ___ ___

1,2 5,3   6,2 6,5 4,4 4,6 3,5   2,2 1,4 2,6 3,3

Get the Point!

Plot each ordered pair and make a point on the chart. Connect all the points to make a picture! The first one is done for you.

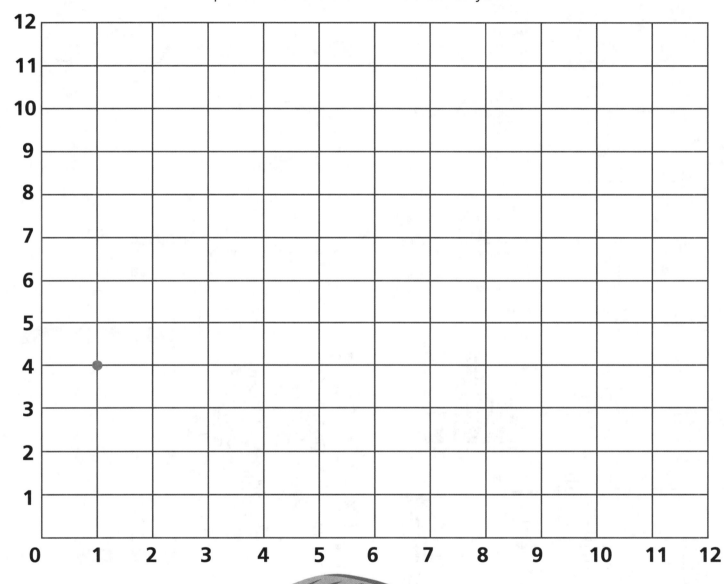

1,4   3,2   5,1

7,2   9,4   5,4

5,7   5,9   5,11

3,9   2,7

Answer Key

Page 4

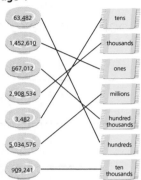

63,482 → hundreds
1,452,610 → millions
667,012 → ones
2,908,534 → hundred thousands
3,482 → tens
5,034,576 → thousands
909,241 → ten thousands

Page 5
2. tens
3. hundred thousands
4. millions
5. thousands
6. hundreds
7. 602
8. 520
9. 3,507
10. 405
11. 46,083
12. 20,394

Page 6
1. <
2. <
3. =
4. <
5. >
6. =
7. >
8. <
9. >
10. <
< 5
> 3
= 2

Page 7
1. 440
2. 2,100
3. 90,000
4. 64,000
5. 300,000
6. 6,000,000
7. tens
8. tens
9. hundreds
10. thousands
11. hundreds
12. tens

Page 8

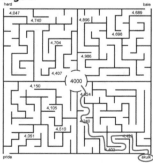

A group of foxes is called a skulk.

Page 9
1. Friday, Tuesday, Thursday, Monday, Wednesday
2. burgers, hot dogs, ice cream bars, cookies, popsicles
3. Ferris wheel
4. red and yellow

Page 10
1. 1,250 feet
2. 1,667 feet
3. 3,666 inches
4. 11,832 inches
5. 20,000 + 9,000 + 30 + 5
6. 20,000 + 300 + 20

Page 11
1. 4,000 + 600 + 50 + 8
2. 30,000 + 3,000 + 400 + 50
3. 800 + 6
4. 100,000 + 20,000 + 6,000 + 800
5. 20,000 + 4,000 + 20 + 7
6. 500,000 + 90,000 + 600 + 2
7. 7,342
8. 528
9. 30,219
10. 1,086
11. 40,396
12. 61,430

Page 12
1. apple, banana, grape, vanilla, berry, coconut
2. three flavors (grape, vanilla, apple)
3. grape, banana, apple
4. vanilla, berry, coconut
5. four flavors (grape, banana, vanilla, berry)

Page 13

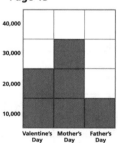

Page 14

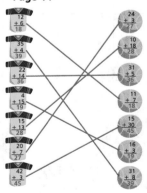

Page 15
1. 9
2. 287
3. 14
4. 379
5. 11
6. 766
7. 16
8. 887
9. 15
10. 897
11. 17
12. 976

Page 16

+ 3	
5	8
4	7
3	6
7	10
9	12

+ 7	
6	13
2	9
1	8
9	16
5	12

+ 1	
8	9
3	4
4	5
7	8
9	10

+ 5	
0	5
6	11
4	9
5	10
8	13

+ 2	
9	11
1	3
2	4
4	6
3	5

Page 17

+ 4	
2	6
6	10
9	13
3	7
4	8

+ 0	
8	8
1	1
7	7
0	0
5	5

+ 6	
3	9
9	15
6	12
2	8
7	13

+ 9	
7	16
2	11
9	18
4	13
5	14

+ 8	
9	17
8	16
5	13
3	11
0	8

Page 18

Page 19
1. 163
2. 133
3. 376
4. 502
5. 150
6. 532
7. 500
8. 861
9. 731
10. 1,150
11. 608
12. 896

Page 20
1. 1600 Pennsylvania Avenue
2. 206 Sixth Avenue
3. 300 Alamo Plaza
4. 233 South Wacker Drive
5. 1313 Harbor Blvd
6. 239 Arch Street

Page 21
1. 560 people
2. 177 butterflies
3. 135 autographs
4. 122 cards

Page 22

Page 23
1. 12
2. 13
3. 32
4. 243
5. 610
6. 323
7. 230
8. 1
9. 143
10. 223
11. 407
12. 363

Page 24

− 3	
8	5
4	1
6	3
10	7
9	6

− 1	
7	6
11	10
3	2
4	3
1	0

− 7	
9	2
10	3
14	7
8	1
13	6

− 9	
18	9
15	6
11	2
13	4
17	8

− 0	
10	10
3	3
1	1
12	12
2	2

Page 25

− 4	
5	1
8	4
10	6
4	0
7	3

− 6	
12	6
14	8
7	1
10	4
9	3

− 2	
5	3
3	1
9	7
7	5
4	2

− 8	
10	2
15	7
9	1
16	8
11	3

− 5	
9	4
15	10
12	7
8	3
10	5

Page 26
2. 8 < 19
3. 27 = 27
4. 28 = 28
5. 48 < 49
6. 17 = 17
< 2
> 1
= 3

Page 27
1. 418
2. 104
3. 54
4. 687
5. 478
6. 278
7. 309
8. 282
9. 79
10. 88
11. 489
12. 177

Page 28
1. 1930
2. 255
3. 100
4. 300
5. 72
6. 16

Page 29
1. 272
2. 59
3. 379
4. 238

Page 30
2. $6 + 5 = 11$
$5 + 6 = 11$
$11 - 5 = 6$
$11 - 6 = 5$
3. $7 + 3 = 10$
$3 + 7 = 10$
$10 - 7 = 3$
$10 - 3 = 7$
4. $9 + 6 = 15$
$6 + 9 = 15$
$15 - 9 = 6$
$15 - 6 = 9$

Page 31
5. $5 + 7 = 12$
$7 + 5 = 12$
$12 - 5 = 7$
$12 - 7 = 5$
6. $5 + 4 = 9$
$4 + 5 = 9$
$9 - 5 = 4$
$9 - 4 = 5$
7. $7 + 6 = 13$
$6 + 7 = 13$
$13 - 7 = 6$
$13 - 6 = 7$
8. $8 + 6 = 14$
$6 + 8 = 14$
$14 - 6 = 8$
$14 - 8 = 6$

Page 32
1. $101 > 69$
2. $421 < 448$
3. $59 < 100$
4. $65 > 43$
5. $289 = 289$
6. $70 < 199$
< 3
> 2
$= 1$

Page 33
1. 635 bottles
2. Zack collected 37 more newspapers.
3. 167 more bottles
4. 18 more boxes

Page 34
1. 750
2. 200 more
3. decrease
4. July and August combined had more campers.
5. June and July

Page 35
1. cookies or brownies
2. cupcakes
3. tarts
4. cookies or brownies
5. lemon bars

Page 36
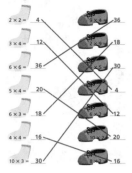

Page 37
1. True
2. True
3. False
4. False
5. True
6. True
7. False
8. True
9. True
10. False
11. True
12. True

Page 38

×2	0	2	4	6	8	10	12	14	16	18	20

×3	0	3	6	9	12	15	18	21	24	27	30

×4	0	4	8	12	16	20	24	28	32	36	40

×5	0	5	10	15	20	25	30	35	40	45	50

Page 39

×6	0	6	12	18	24	30	36	42	48	54	60

×7	0	7	14	21	28	35	42	49	56	63	70

×8	0	8	16	24	32	40	48	56	64	72	80

×9	0	9	18	27	36	45	54	63	72	81	90

×10	0	10	20	30	40	50	60	70	80	90	100

Page 40
1. $48 < 50$
2. $55 > 36$
3. $40 = 40$
4. $28 < 39$
5. $24 < 33$
6. $26 < 30$
> 1
< 4
$= 1$

Page 41
1. 64
2. 256
3. 252
4. 162
5. 177
6. 146
7. 104
8. 162
9. 490
10. 528
11. 387
12. 392

Page 42
1. 476
2. 1492
3. 1776
4. 776 BCE
5. 1863
6. 1969

Page 43
1. 198 seats
2. 240 people
3. 21 miles
4. 30 fish

Page 44
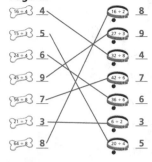

3. 19 baskets
4. 9 sundaes

Page 45
1. True
2. False
3. False
4. True
5. False
6. True
7. True
8. True
9. False
10. True
11. False
12. True

Page 46

÷2	7	4	6	9	8	5	3	2	1	10

÷3	6	9	10	3	7	5	4	8	2	1

÷4	5	9	2	3	6	4	7	1	8	10

÷5	2	10	7	4	3	9	5	8	6	1

Page 47

÷6	3	4	6	9	7	5	8	10	1	2

÷7	7	10	3	5	9	2	1	6	4	8

÷8	10	4	5	3	2	9	1	6	8	7

÷9	8	3	6	2	7	4	10	9	1	5

÷10	3	4	6	10	5	8	2	1	9	7

Page 48

Page 49
1. 44 R3
2. 104 R4
3. 234 R2
4. 252 R1
5. 11 R7
6. 231 R2
7. 34 R2
8. 73 R5
9. 14 R1
10. 37 R1
11. 35 R8
12. 41 R5

Page 50
2. 173 R4
3. 13 R9
4. 93 R2
5. 38 R1
6. 25 R3
In 2004 kids from all over the world gathered to make the world's longest line of footprints. There were 10,932 footprints in the line.

Page 51
1. 32 peas
2. 2 cubes

Page 52
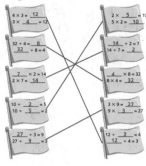

Page 53
1. 175
2. 104
3. 732
4. 23 R2
5. 172 R1
6. 322
7. 1830
8. 226 R2
9. 420
10. 35
11. 6510
12. 36 R1

Page 54
1. $5 \times 3 = 15$
2. $12 \div 3 = 4$
3. $7 \times 2 = 14$
4. $8 \times 9 = 72$
5. $35 \div 7 = 5$
6. $24 \div 8 = 3$
7. $4 \times 6 = 24$
8. $3 \times 9 = 27$
9. $6 \times 8 = 48$

× = 6   ÷ = 3

Page 55
1. 48 days
2. 25 groups
3. 13 rows
4. 576 tickets

Page 56
1. Ruby and Natalie
2. 20 books
3. 20 books
4. Jack
5. Ashley

Page 57
1. 12
2. Star
3. 27
4. 2
5. 22 students

Page 58
1. $\frac{1}{4}$
2. $\frac{3}{4}$
3. $\frac{2}{5}$
4. $\frac{1}{2}$
5. $\frac{2}{3}$
6. $\frac{1}{3}$

Page 59
1. $\frac{3}{4}$
2. $\frac{3}{8}$
3. $\frac{7}{10}$
4. $\frac{3}{5}$
5. $\frac{1}{2}$
6. $\frac{1}{6}$
7.
8.
9.

Page 60
2. $\frac{3}{6} = \frac{2}{4}$
3. $\frac{2}{3} > \frac{1}{6}$
4. $\frac{5}{6} > \frac{1}{3}$
5. $\frac{2}{5} < \frac{3}{5}$
6. $\frac{1}{2} > \frac{1}{3}$

Page 61
1. $\frac{2}{4}$ or $\frac{1}{2}$
2. $\frac{2}{3}$
3. $\frac{2}{5}$
4. $\frac{5}{8}$
5. $\frac{4}{10}$ or $\frac{2}{5}$
6. $\frac{4}{7}$
7. $\frac{5}{6}$
8. $\frac{5}{8}$
9. $\frac{5}{7}$
10. $\frac{6}{8}$ or $\frac{3}{4}$
11. $\frac{9}{10}$
12. $\frac{2}{9}$

Page 62

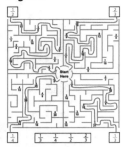

Page 63
1. $8.25	7. $7.26
2. $0.74	8. $128.05
3. $7.25	9. $9.13
4. $7.88	10. $7.01
5. $6.74	11. $221.45
6. $4.62	12. $74.50

Page 64
1. $15.1 million
2. $0.05
3. $1.50
4. $99.00
5. $0.01
6. $0.02

Page 65
1. $0.75
2. $0.05
3. A ten-dollar bill
4. $9.00

Page 66

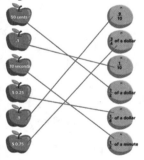

Page 67
1. $8.10	7. $6.01
2. $0.25	8. $14.20
3. $42.00	9. $0.85
4. $3.75	10. $5.97
5. $0.08	11. $11.21
6. $2.75	12. $6.68

Page 68
1. chocolate bars and bubble gum

2. $\frac{1}{6}$

3. $\frac{3}{6}$ or $\frac{1}{2}$

4. $\frac{5}{6}$

5. lollipops and lemon drops

Page 69
1. $0.10
2. $18.80
3. $ 0.85
4. $ 0.70
5. 5 cents

Page 70

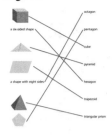

Page 71
2. 18 = 18
3. 11 > 8
4. 12 < 14
5. 20 = 20
6. 16 > 15

Page 72
1. 6 feet^2
2. 15 feet^2
3. 6 feet^3
4. 12 feet^3

Page 73
1. 24 feet
2. 25 square feet
3. Yes, they will have 12 square feet together.
4. 36 feet^3

Page 74
1. equilateral	6. equilateral
2. right	7. right
3. equilateral	8. isosceles
4. isosceles	9. isosceles
5. right	

Page 75

Page 76
1. grams	6. ruler
2. tons	7. feet
3. centimeters	8. inches
4. pounds	9. scale
5. ounces	

Page 77
1. 2 hours = 120 minutes
2. 24 inches = 2 feet
3. 2 yards = 6 feet
4. 3 feet = 36 inches
5. 180 minutes = 3 hours
6. 2 meters = 200 centimeters
7. 36 inches = 1 yard
8. 300 centimeters = 3 meters
9. 4 hours = 240 minutes
10. 5 meters = 500 centimeters
11. 120 minutes = 2 hours
12. 9 feet = 3 yards

Page 78

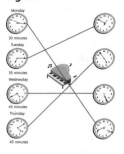

Page 79
1. 4:20	3. 5:40
2. 4 feet × 4 feet	4. 2 spools

Page 80
1. 16 feet^2
2. 16 feet
3. 4 feet^2
4. 48 inches
5. 8 feet

Page 81
1. Fairytale Friends
2. Amy's Adventures and Baking with Bonnie are both 30 minutes long
3. 15 minutes longer
4. Fairytale Friends
5. Fairytale Friends, The Spooky House, Animal Antics

Page 82

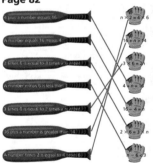

Page 83
1. 12	7. 24
2. 4	8. 16
3. 2	9. 16
4. 15	10. 5
5. 13	11. 7
6. 10	12. 22

Page 84
1. +	8. ×
2. ×	9. ÷
3. +	10. ÷
4. −	+ 2
5. ÷	− 2
6. ÷	× 2
7. −	÷ 4

Page 85
1. 12	7. 5
2. 3	8. 2
3. 19	9. 5
4. 8	10. 5
5. 4	11. 10
6. 6	12. 21

Page 86

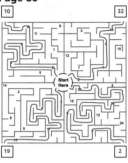

Page 87
1. 54	7. 40
2. 6	8. 5
3. 30	9. 12
4. 35	10. 48
5. 96	11. 10
6. 60	12. 30

Page 88
1. 40 ÷ 8	4. 48 + 40
2. 40 × 8	5. 4 × 8
3. 8 ÷ 4	6. 40 − 8

Page 89
1. The 70 page notebook for $1.40. (The cost is only 2 cents per sheet.)
2. He would spend the least amount at the store.
3. $ 7.50
4. $15.00

Page 90
1. b	4. c
2. a	5. c
3. c	

Page 91

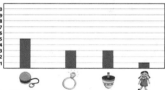

1. 10
2. toy rings
3. 4
4. There was 1 yo-yo and 1 doll left.

Page 92
Why was the student rushing to find all the ordered pairs?
He was late for an appointment.

Page 93

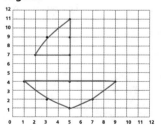